# The Cost of Service

**M. Anthony Garner**

Imminent Storm Publishing
P.O. 452
Houma, Louisiana 70361-0452

## ABSTRACT

*The Cost of Service* reveals the profound personal and collective sacrifices made by individuals in law enforcement, ministry, and the military. It shines a light on the emotional, spiritual, and relational toll their service demands. This book also gives voice to the families who stand behind them—those who support their loved ones and quietly carry the weight of duty. Told through authentic stories and candid reflections, it explores the cost of living a life devoted to others.

A deeply patriotic work, *The Cost of Service* honors the tenacity, mission, and unwavering strength of those who have served.

# The Cost of Service

The Cost of Service.

Copyright © 2025 by Michael Anthony Garner

All rights reserved. No part of this book may be reproduced or transmitted in any form or by any means without written permission from the author.
Printed in the United States.

Hardback ISBN: 979-8-9893592-4-0
Paperback ISBN: 979-8-9893592-5-7
Audiobook ISBN: 979-8-9893592-6-4
E-Book ISBN: 979-8-9893592-7-1

Published in USA by Imminent Storm Publishing

# The Cost of Service

## Dedication

This book is dedicated to the men and women who have selflessly given their time and lives to serve in military service, law enforcement, and church ministry. Much attention has been given to the overwhelming number of law enforcement professionals, military service members, and veterans who tragically take their own lives. Yet few have addressed the immense stress and silent suffering within church ministry. I also dedicate this book to those who have embraced the call to ministry—often at great personal cost. Society has come to expect an unshakable standard of endurance from those who serve, often overlooking their very real and fragile humanity.

"The privilege of service is seldom achieved without sacrifice. A heart of service is one that acknowledges the potential for sacrifice—yet still continues."

—M. Anthony Garner

# The Cost of Service

## TABLE OF CONTENTS

| | |
|---|---|
| Preface | 6 |
| Introduction | 9 |
| Chapter One | 12 |
|     Called to Serve, Bound to Sacrifice | 12 |
| Chapter Two | 23 |
|     The Uniform and the Collar | 23 |
| Chapter Three | 33 |
|     Behind the Badge, Beyond the Pulpit | 33 |
| Chapter Four | 43 |
|     Invisible Wounds | 43 |
| Chapter Five | 54 |
|     Faith under Fire | 54 |
| Chapter Six | 63 |
|     The Weight of the Fallen | 63 |
| Chapter Seven | 71 |
|     Families on the Front Line | 71 |
| Chapter Eight | 80 |
|     Crossroads of Justice and Grace | 80 |
| Chapter Nine | 89 |
|     When the Mission Ends | 89 |
| Chapter Ten | 99 |
|     Redemption through the Call | 99 |

| | |
|---|---|
| References | 110 |
| THE FINAL CALL | 112 |
| ACKNOWLEDGMENTS | 113 |

## Preface

This book began as a silent burden—one that grew heavier year after year with the weight of the work. As a veteran, a law enforcement officer, and a worship leader, I have witnessed the burdens that those who answer the call to serve carry on their shoulders every day. I have seen the bravery and sense of calling that define these roles, but I have also seen—and personally experienced—the suffering that lingers long after the mission is completed, the shift has ended, or the sermon is preached.

*The Cost of Service* is not a political statement, a theological essay, or a plea for pity. It is an honest reflection on what a life of service truly entails—whether in the military, in law enforcement, or in ministry—and the sacrifices required along the way. These roles are often praised publicly, but seldom fully understood in private. We admire the accomplishments, yet rarely comprehend the cost.

This book is for those who wear the uniform and for

## The Cost of Service

those who stand beside them. It is for the husbands and wives, the children, the friends, and the congregations who wonder what lies beneath the silence of the people they love.

Who is it for? It is for all who have long struggled to reconcile a higher calling with their own personal path of suffering.

The stories and reflections in these pages come from real events—some my own, and others shared with me by men and women whose lives have been profoundly shaped by service. These stories are not always easy to tell or to find. They are stories of courage, yes—but also of trauma, loss, doubt, and redemption. They reveal the messiness of a life that is both sacred and costly.

I wrote this book because these stories matter. Because the invisible wounds deserve attention. Because service—whatever form it takes—should be honored not only for its heroism, but for its humanity. If you see yourself in these pages, know that you are not alone. If you are reading to

# The Cost of Service

understand someone you love, I hope this book becomes a beacon of clarity, compassion, and connection.

# The Cost of Service

## Introduction

Service, at its core, is a high-sounding ideal—often wrapped in noble words like *honor*, *duty*, and *sacrifice*. We pay tribute to those in uniform, whether they wear the camouflage of a soldier, the badge of a local police officer, or the robes of a reverend. We honor their commitment to something greater than themselves: defending freedom, protecting communities, and guiding souls.

But behind the ceremonies, mottos, and quiet pride of service lies an uncomfortable and often unseen truth—the personal cost of service on a deeply human level. This book was born from that silent truth.

It is a pilgrimage into the lives of those who have chosen paths that demand more than skill, more than knowledge—they demand the full depths and heights of mind, heart, and soul. To join the military is to march toward danger, possibly with no

## The Cost of Service

return. To become a police officer is to face the worst of humanity day after day. To minister in the church is to carry the burdens of others while privately wrestling with your own. True service, when taken seriously in any of these forms, is not merely a role. It is a weight.

*The Cost of Service* is not written to diminish the valor within these callings. Rather, it seeks to highlight the truth that honor is often born out of hardship. This is a book for the men and women who serve or have served our country—and for the ones who love them. It is both a reflection on what is lost and a meditation on what is gained. It is about the trauma that lingers, the faith that falters, and the grace that proves itself powerful.

These pages will peel back the proverbial scab and examine the gritty, dark, and deeply human side of service. We will face the emotional wounds of battle, the moral injuries of policing a broken world, and the quiet suffering of spiritual leaders. Yet, we will also lift up the resilience, purpose, and

## The Cost of Service

hope that can emerge when we choose to count the cost—and still answer the call.

I will speak candidly about personal struggles. While I will not mention names, those involved will likely recognize the events. This is not an attempt to indict anyone's actions or inactions. Rather, it is a collection of real-life experiences intended to remind the reader: *You are not alone.* To serve is to offer oneself. To appreciate that service is to honor it more deeply. This is the soul of *The Cost of Service*.

# The Cost of Service

## Chapter One

Called to Serve, Bound to Sacrifice

> "Public service must be more than doing a job efficiently and honestly. It must be a complete dedication to the people and to the nation."
>
> Margaret Chase Smith

My call to serve began early in life—at a time when I was scarcely old enough to understand what a "calling" truly was. I vividly remember, at just seven years old, telling my mom that God had called me to preach. I had no idea what that meant, or the weight those words carried. But I can assure you—my mom never let me forget it. I am sure some of you have those seemingly small childhood declarations your parents never let you live down. That was mine.

**"A thread connects warrior, peacekeeper, and worshiper, a calling greater than individual ambition."**

By age thirteen, I had learned to play the piano by ear, which quickly led to me playing the organ at my church. Music had always been a part of my life. Since I was about five

# The Cost of Service

years old, I thought I was Michael Jackson. I mean, we shared the same first name—so it had to be destiny, right? With my mom serving as choir director, my siblings and I all did our "tour of duty" in the church choir. It was expected. It was normal. It was the start of something deeper.

When I turned seventeen, I began considering military service. Although my grades were decent and I had received an engineering scholarship from Southern University in Baton Rouge (SUBR), I was looking for a way to get out—to escape and start something new. I initially visited the Army recruiter and asked about becoming a Green Beret. Since I was still under eighteen, a parent or guardian would have to sign a consent form for me to enlist.

The recruiter played a VHS promotional tape showcasing Green Beret training, thinking it would help convince her. It had the opposite effect. The recruiter explained that her "baby boy" would be handed a raw chicken and a knife, dropped in the middle of the woods, and told to find his way

## The Cost of Service

back to base. My mom looked at him, looked at me, and said a firm, immediate, "No."

Needless to say, I did not join the Army. Instead, I enrolled at Southern. While on campus, I joined the Naval Reserve Officer Training Corps (NROTC) program. But after just a semester and a half, I made a decision that would shape the trajectory of my life: I joined the finest fighting force in the world—the United States Marine Corps. That decision took me from the streets of southern Louisiana all the way to the Persian Gulf.

Growing up in the Uptown (UPT) and Hollygrove areas of New Orleans, I never had dreams of becoming a police officer. In fact, I hated the police. My grandmother lived on Martin Luther King Boulevard, right across from the Melpomene Housing Projects—known to locals as "The MELF." During visits, I often witnessed members of the New Orleans Police Department (NOPD) "put in work" on residents who looked just like me.

# The Cost of Service

Ritz et al. (2020) assert that those in public service act with the ideal of serving the public interest. Though our uniforms and missions may differ, we are often drawn to military service, law enforcement, or ministry by a similar internal summons—an impulse to protect, lead, serve, and uphold what is good.

Whether standing watch in a war-torn land, patrolling an anxious city, or leading in houses of worship, these servants of society answer not only to man, but to their conscience— and often, to God. For many, the call to serve begins with a crystalline moment: an encounter, a tragedy, or a quiet whisper from the soul saying, *"This is what you were made for."* It is rarely a calculated career decision. More often, it springs from a deep, internal desire to sacrifice oneself for something greater.

In the military, that sense of duty is sharpened by the realization that freedom demands sacrifice. Soldiers are not merely trained to fight—they are trained to uphold the

## The Cost of Service

principles that define a nation. Within law enforcement, duty is rooted in justice and public safety, and in a silent pledge to run toward danger when others run away. The calling to ministry is spiritual in nature. It is a commitment to lead others into the presence of the divine, to guide hearts toward hope, truth, and transformation. Yet whether it is the wound in the body of a soldier, the wound in the soul of a nation plagued by the horrors of war, or the spiritual wound in the one who bears it— these scars are not always visible.

Sleepless nights, survivor's remorse, and the endless echoes of what has been seen and done become burdens carried long after the service is rendered. These men and women live under constant pressure—second-guessing decisions in a world quick to judge and slow to understand. The weight of navigating danger, bureaucracy, and public scrutiny erodes the soul in ways few professions can comprehend. Their families endure a silent dread every time a uniform is worn. A badge may earn respect, but it can also attract danger— both physical

# The Cost of Service

and moral.

Behind the medals, uniforms, and Sunday smiles are silent sacrifices. Long hours and emotional walls strain marriages. Children grow up missing birthdays and holidays. Personal struggles are hidden, because struggle is too often seen as weakness.

Ames et al. (2021) describe *moral injury* as spiritual, psychological, and moral distress—a soul-deep wound. Though commonly applied to combat veterans, moral injury also haunts police officers and ministers. It is the lasting pain of doing what had to be done, knowing it cannot be undone. Whether pulling a trigger or enforcing a law that seems unjust, the weight is crushing. Isolation—emotional, relational, and spiritual—is one of its most frequent costs.

Not many know what it is like to hold a dying friend in their arms—or to pray with someone moments before they take their own life. Only a remnant can sit with you in the silence that follows. As Pollock and Augusto (2023) note, personal

## The Cost of Service

relationships can either enhance or detract from stress buffering and resilience. When those relationships are strained or absent, the weight becomes even harder to bear.

Few outsiders recognize the emotional and spiritual burdens carried by worship leaders and ministers. Instead, these leaders often absorb the grief of the broken, the doubts of the searching, and the conflicts of community life. Theirs is a vocation of relentless giving, and the line between sacred duty and personal burnout is dangerously thin. When faith falters—or when the institution they serve fails them—the resulting wounds can be spiritual, even existential.

Across all types of service, a common thread emerges: *loneliness.* Duty has a way of separating those who serve from those who do not. Friends may not understand. Family members might resent the long hours, the missed birthdays, and the ever-present risk.

**"True selflessness cannot exist in the realm of selfishness."**

# The Cost of Service

If the servant reveals exhaustion or uncertainty, it may be perceived as an abandonment of the mission, the team, or even their faith. The temptation, then, is to push through—concealing the cost, wearing the armor even when off duty. But this silence only deepens the wounds. Yet, even in adversity, there is something sacred about giving.

Sacrifice—when born of duty and love—has the power to transform pain into purpose. Each deployment, each patrol, and each sermon is an offering. The cost is not too much to pay when it is part of a greater story. Through service, we often learn from one another where to draw strength—a touch on the shoulder from a fellow soldier, a wordless nod to a partner before a call, or a tearful thank-you from a congregant after worship. These quiet affirmations are what sustain them.

Faith is powerful in that way. For many, service is not just a duty to country, community, or church—it is a duty to God. That faith sanctifies the sacrifice, offering both meaning and redemption. By faith, the wounded are made whole. In

## The Cost of Service

faith, the tired find rest—in the presence of God and in the community that walks beside them.

To serve is to give, and to give is to risk loss. But in that giving, something timeless is born. The world will always need those who are willing to stand and fight when others are afraid to move. The true test is whether you are willing to pay the price—not for glory, but for good. True selflessness cannot survive in the soil of selfishness.

The soldier, the officer, and the minister each carry the weight of their calling in different ways. Yet all share a common readiness to serve beyond themselves. In that service, they offer the world a truth too often forgotten: courage, sacrifice, and service are the highest forms of love. Real. Costly. Relentless and always—*worth the price.*

The Bible is not shy about the price of a calling. Moses knew the weight of leading people who did not want to be led. David battled giants—both on the battlefield and within his own soul. Paul endured chains, whippings, and rejection for the sake

# The Cost of Service

of the gospel.

Christ gave everything—even His life—in service. Jesus said, *"Greater love hath no man than this, that a man lay down his life for his friends"* (John 15:13, KJV). Not every soldier, officer, or minister in uniform dies bodily. Many of us die emotionally, spiritually, and relationally—*every single day.*

The Apostle Paul urges believers to *"present your bodies a living sacrifice, holy, acceptable unto God, which is your reasonable service"* (Romans 12:1, KJV). At its core, worship is service. It is the daily death of comfort for the good of others. Service demands a high cost—but it also opens the door to deep rewards: purpose, camaraderie, and the quiet, moral satisfaction of knowing you stood in the gap. Still, those who serve must also learn to receive. Healing comes through community, therapy, prayer—and time. We must come to understand that rest is not weakness. Rest is obedience.

When Elijah, having just called down fire from heaven and confronted evil, collapsed beneath a broom tree and asked

# The Cost of Service

to die (1 Kings 19), God did not rebuke him. Instead, He sent an angel to feed him and give him rest. Even prophets need sleep. Sadly, this is a lesson many of us ignore in pursuit of mission accomplishment, case resolution, or the next move of God.

To serve is to carry a weight that can be crushing—but also sacred. Whether in boots, beneath a badge, or behind a pulpit, those who are called are marked. Not because they are stronger, but because they are *willing*—willing to show up, to stand guard, to lift others. They do not do it to be seen. They do it because something deep within *commands* them. While the cost is very real, so is the promise: *"They that sow in tears shall reap in joy"* (Psalm 126:5, KJV). In the end, the world is changed not by the celebrated, but by the dedicated—by those who hear the call, count the cost, and go.... nonetheless.

# The Cost of Service

## Chapter Two

### The Uniform and the Collar

"The best way to find yourself is to lose yourself in the service of others."

Mahatma Gandhi

I have walked each of the three roads: one in desert boots, one in shined duty shoes, and one in the "sandals" of worship. **"It follows us home, in our relationships, our sleep, and our prayers."** We carry firearms, radios, and Bibles. We may battle in distant lands, patrol city streets, or minister to weary souls. Yet beneath the veneer of our respective uniforms lies a shared burden: the weight of responsibility, the aftermath of human destruction, and the constant tension of being both strong and fragile. Though the armed forces, law enforcement, and ministry occupy three distinct worlds, the hearts of those who serve in them beat in remarkable unison.

Each of these callings rests on one inconvenient truth: we are responsible for other people's lives, safety, and souls. These are not small things. As a military veteran, I can say

## The Cost of Service

firsthand—this responsibility is not theoretical; it is tangible. The success of a mission can hinge on the smallest of actions. I have heard Marines say, *"I'm carrying more than my weapon—I'm carrying my squad's lives."* One mistake, one misstep, and someone does not make it home. Let that sink in.

In law enforcement, those tasked with keeping the peace face a similar tension—every shift presents a fork in the road. A traffic stop can end in a handshake—or in gunfire. Officers must read people in a matter of seconds, often without the full story. If that judgment is wrong, someone can get hurt—or we may not come home at all.

In ministry, the burden is more spiritual—but no less heavy. There is always that quiet wondering after every worship service: *Did those in the back row hear enough hope to change their lives? Did the worship music complement the message? Was the selection of songs diverse and meaningful enough?*

# The Cost of Service

The pulpit can feel leaden, even during moments that appear joyful.

> "I have seen children in handcuffs one day and later in caskets."

It is both a privilege and a shared weight—to care for the souls of others. Yet the pressure does not remain on the field, the beat, or the platform. It follows us home. It lives in our relationships, our sleep, and our prayers.

I have been both blessed and burdened to walk in these professions. Though rarely taught or openly acknowledged in society, those of us in these roles often become unexpected authorities on human suffering. Service members encounter the grim realities of war— children used as human shields, friends killed by unseen enemies, and ethical dilemmas for which even the best training cannot prepare us. What is seen cannot be unseen and what is unseen often goes unhealed.

The officer works in spaces where violence, addiction, and poverty intertwine. I have seen children in handcuffs one day and in caskets the next. It is a disheartening reality—one that hits even harder when those children are your own family

## The Cost of Service

members. At times, we collectively wonder if we are making any difference at all.

The minister walks alongside the bereaved, the addicted, the suicidal, and the betrayed. As a music minister, I once had a pastor falsely accuse me of adultery—because *he* had been caught in an adulterous affair and needed a distraction. I had done no such thing. Eventually, the truth came to light, and the pastor was removed, but the emotional toll was undeniable. Ministers absorb the tears of shattered marriages, the whispered admissions of shame, and the cries of people broken by life and, sometimes, by faith. We are expected to face suffering again and again—and still show up the next day with an open heart and an intact soul.

Public perception has always shaped how we are seen. Soldiers are heroes—until the politics change. Police are protectors—until one viral video paints the entire profession with a single brush. Ministers are shepherds—until they show they are *human*, and for whatever reason, can no longer be

# The Cost of Service

*superhuman.*

All three professions—military, law enforcement, and ministry—exist in the tension between public trust and public suspicion. There is a constant pressure to be moral: morally self-righteous, morally strong, and morally unshakable. When we fall, we often fall hard—and alone. Many of us live with the belief that we are only as good as our last decision. There is little room for doubt, and even less room to fall apart in the roles we carry. The burden of being seen as the example, the rock, and the leader—it wears on the soul.

Ministers, too, face their own spiritual challenges. I have had moments where I feared that mourning too loudly or questioning too openly would cause others to think I had lost my faith. So, I would sit in silence, keep my mouth shut—and slowly die inside. Sometimes, the deepest wounds are inflicted in the very place we go to be healed.

I once went through a particularly difficult experience involving a Christian play I had written called *Choices*. It was

## The Cost of Service

crafted to reach youth through relatable dialogue and real-life scenarios. My church had a tradition of producing theatrical outreach during Easter and Christmas—with full participation and a dedicated budget. But for this youth production, there was no such support. No budget. No tangible ministerial backing. We struggled to find props, resources, and the presence of leadership.

To make matters worse, one of the lead teen actors, whom I loved dearly, was repeatedly missing rehearsals. Wanting to ensure a successful performance, I made the decision to move forward with the understudy. Not long after, I was summoned to the pastor's office and told that I could not simply replace the teen—because their parents had complained, and they were considered "good" members of the church. Out of obedience to my pastor, I reinstated the original teen—despite believing it was unfair to the rest of the cast who had shown up, practiced, and given their best. Between the inconsistent support, difficult parent interactions, and ministerial oversight

## The Cost of Service

without participation, I found myself emotionally drained. I remember standing in the living room of a trusted prayer leader—crying, broken, and overwhelmed.

At this point, I felt broken. I did not know if the lack of support was because the effort was *my* idea and not an official church initiative, or if the church simply was not interested in reaching the teenagers we hoped to impact. Whatever the reason, creating a meaningful and spiritually resonant production became an emotionally and spiritually exhausting task. Still, the play was successful. Because I must be a glutton for pain, we presented the play twice—in separate years. In both performances, we faced the *exact same* lack of support.

In each of these callings—military, law enforcement, ministry—roles that are meant to be grounded in community, teamwork, and congregation, one can feel profoundly alone. To whom does the guardian turn when the guardian needs a guardian? Who counsels the counselor? Who comforts the comforter?

## The Cost of Service

Returning soldiers often wrestle with emotional detachment. The lament is common: *No one recognizes what we've been through.* The badge, once a symbol of honor, can become a wall. Ministers—though surrounded by people—can feel like they live in glass houses: visible to everyone, but truly known by almost no one.

This isolation is dangerous. It tends to make seeking help feel like an admission of weakness. It can lead to burnout, moral failure, or despair. The fact that high suicide rates persist in at least two of the three fields, are an indictment of the soul-crushing silence many bear.

Petersen et al. (2024) tell us that nearly 600 service members and 6000 veterans die by suicide every year. Based on studies, Violanti (2022) asserts law enforcement are 54% more likely to die by suicide than people in other jobs. Though there is limited data on suicide in the ministry, I have known a pastor who committed suicide. In the midst of the weight, there is a redemptive strand as well.

## The Cost of Service

The sacrifices are not for nothing. When soldiers protect the innocent, when officers restore peace, and when ministers breathe life into the broken, they are participating in something divine. These callings do not simply bear the weight of a broken world—they carry within them the possibility of its healing.

Those who serve understand better than most the paradox of strength and submission. If we can learn to meet one another across roles—across uniforms and responsibilities—we may find ourselves walking a shared path toward deeper connection and collective restoration. There is strength in shared suffering. Perhaps the most important truth to hold onto is this: you are not alone.

Imagine this: a round table. Not a circle of soldiers trading war stories, but a sacred space of listening. A chaplain. A Marine. A police officer. Seated together—not to compare burdens, but to bear them together. To pray. To admit we are weary. To confess we are human. To acknowledge we *need* one another. This is how healing begins—not by suppressing the

## The Cost of Service

burden, but by sharing it. As Galatians 6:2 (KJV) reminds us: "Bear ye one another's burdens, and so fulfil the law of Christ."

Imagine if military units, precincts, church communities knew this truth, not just in theory, but in practice? What if we constructed some bridges for our ministers and counselors to acknowledge each other, recognizing that though we serve in different jobs, our souls wail in the same fashion? A burden shared is a strength shared. In a world that forgets about the price of service, maybe that is the most important gift we can give each other: the tenderness of the vision and the intimacy within us.

# The Cost of Service

## Chapter Three

### Behind the Badge, Beyond the Pulpit

> "The battles that count aren't the ones for gold medals. The struggles within yourself - the invisible, inevitable battles inside all of us - that's where it's at."
>
> Jesse Owens

They are us—policemen, soldiers, and preachers. Protectors of our safety and pastors of our souls. We watch them in uniform and behind microphones—standing tall, speaking with authority, bringing order to moments of chaos. They are the ones we turn to when the world collapses. But seldom do we pause to ask: Who do *they* turn to? Who do *they* call when their world falls apart?

Behind the uniform shirt and out from behind the pulpit— beyond the air of confidence and the steady voice—they are human beings. Human beings who often carry silent struggles so deep, they no longer know where to place them. The weight is real. The cost is high. Unfortunately, the public rarely sees that.

# The Cost of Service

**"Vulnerability becomes a privilege for which only a small subset of people feel secure enough to pay."**

Military and police personnel, as well as ministers, often feel that life is a performance. Every action is under scrutiny. Every word carries weight. There is little margin for error. The badge and the uniform represent authority. The pulpit represents morality.

To fall is to risk credibility—and for some, their very livelihood. A minister can lead worship, preach a funeral in the morning, counsel a suicidal teenager at noon, and teach a marriage class in the evening. If they stumble once—say the wrong thing, seem too tired, and show too much emotion on a Sunday— that is what people remember.

Officers know a similar reality. It is an unspoken rule: you can do a thousand things right, but if you make *one* mistake, if *one* moment is caught on tape, you're no longer the cop— you're the bad guy. What gets overlooked is that these men and women are also fathers, mothers, sons, daughters—*human beings*. This kind of visibility creates pressure that builds

## The Cost of Service

emotional walls. Vulnerability becomes a luxury only a few feel safe enough to afford. Most who serve endure in silence.

What happens when the wound is *from within*? I once volunteered for a brand-new program being launched by the department I worked for. In the beginning, it was just me and one other officer. Unfortunately, the program stalled shortly after we signed up. Two years later, it resurfaced. By then, the other officer had transferred to another division for a promotion, so I restated my interest—this time with a new officer.

When the department began scheduling volunteers for training, I was informed that my slot had been given to someone else. I was also told that the new officer would attend the training, but I would not be part of the program at all. When I asked why, my supervisor told me that, after speaking with his superior, they had decided it was not in the agency's "long-term best interest" to send me.

Since this was the only explanation I was given, I was left to assume the root reason. I was not the same race as the

## The Cost of Service

other officer, and I was older than the other officer. The root reason could either be racism or ageism. I was noticeably angry as I had volunteered for numerous assignments within the department and felt slighted to say the least.

Within a year of completing his training, the other officer applied for and was hired by another agency. This created a vacancy in the very program I was once denied. My supervisor came to me and asked if I was interested in joining the program. I respectfully replied, *"I'm good."* My reasoning was simple: if I was not the best choice for the department's "long-term interest" a year ago, why would I be now? The answer, of course, was need. A favored candidate had left, and now the department needed someone to fill the gap. I remembered how quickly I had been overlooked and that memory stayed with me.

Emotions can be repressed in any line of work—for the sake of others. Officers and veterans are trained to detach quickly from tragic scenes: war zones, car accidents, child abuse, and domestic violence. Pastors carry the grief of their

## The Cost of Service

congregation week after week, often absorbing pain with no outlet of their own.

This emotional price adds up. Suppression becomes muscle memory and the collapse doesn't always look like a dramatic breakdown. Sometimes it's more subtle: insomnia, irritability, social withdrawal, or the slow erosion that comes from numbing behaviors—drinking, overworking, and disengaging from family.

The military, ministry, and law enforcement all share a rhythm of irregular schedules, constant chaos, and emotional depletion. These demands inevitably bleed into home life. The spouse of a police officer lives with a quiet, constant fear: *Will they come home at the end of this shift?*

In New Orleans, in December 2015—before my wife and I were married—the police vehicle I was in was shot into four times while following a stolen vehicle. The news coverage quickly blasted the headline: *Unmarked State Police Unit Involved in Shooting.* My then-girlfriend had the *Find My Friends* app on

# The Cost of Service

her phone and used it to check my location. It showed me at University Medical Center (UMC). What she didn't yet know was that, after a traumatic incident, it is standard protocol for officers to be checked out at the hospital. All she saw was my name and my location in the app—and a shooting on the news. What would your immediate thought be?

A pastor's children may give up weekends, privacy even parental attention for the church. It is not rare for a minister's spouse to love the church and despise the way it always succeeds in coming first. The minister may be torn between guilt and obligation, and think that they never wanted to put their kids second to ministry. It can feel that way sometimes.

Depression, Post-Traumatic Stress Disorder (PTSD), and suicide rates among police officers and military veterans are far above the national average. The stoic culture in each profession often presents as a limitation to early intercession. I have driven home in silence, head down, looking at my steering wheel and wondered what it would be like to just not wake up. I did not say anything. I thought, "I am the military veteran and the good police officer, and I am part of my church worship team." I believed those who lead do not break.

Ministers are called to walk by faith—not only as part of their job description, but as a necessity for their own survival. Their livelihood and their soul both hinge on it. So, when doubt creeps in, it can feel like betrayal. The truth is: doubt is deeply human. Every one of us wrestles with it, no matter our role or title.

I have gone through seasons when I could not pray. As a worship leader, I was leading others into God's presence—while I had not truly been there myself in months. I was hollow inside. Who could I tell? I was walking through a spiritual drought, but the idea of vulnerability felt... *off*. Would people think it was strange? Would they lose confidence in me if I admitted I was struggling?

Police officers, too, are subject to spiritual conflict. Faced every day with the worst that human beings are capable of,

## The Cost of Service

many struggle with profound theological questions: Where is God in this? Why does evil keep winning? These challenges often remain unspoken in the department. One common theme among people from these professions is that they can never actually relax. I still, off duty and after my military service, scan every crowd and every room. It is hard to turn it off.

Some pastors check back in even while they are on vacation. Someone always needs prayer. Rest feels selfish. Devoting time to self-care seems like a dereliction of duty. Then the cycle persists into weariness, spiritually, emotionally, and physically.

There is a perilous point at which the role turns into the individual. The badge, the uniform, the pulpit—they are no longer *part* of who you are. They become *all* of who you are. That is why burnout hits so hard. It is not just about losing energy or motivation. It is the deeper fear: *"If I can't do this... then who am I?"*

This identity crisis is a silent epidemic. It leads to quiet

## The Cost of Service

resignations, emotional isolation—and sometimes, tragedy. Healing begins with safe spaces. Spaces where officers, veterans, and ministers can finally take off the armor and speak without judgment. Support groups. Counseling. Retreats intentionally designed for those in these professions.

These can offer the first breath of relief. The first honest conversation. The first step toward recovery.

In order to heal, a cultural change is needed. A shift that says being tired, having doubt, and asking for help, is alright. Strength is not the absence of difficulty; it is the determination to overcome it. The Bible reminds us that God sees us even in our hidden places: *"Yea, the darkness hideth not from thee; but the night shineth as the day: the darkness and the light are both alike to thee"* (Psalm 139:12, KJV).

God sees through the parts of ourselves we cover with badges, uniforms, and pulpits. He does not flinch. Our fatigue, our disappointment—these do not drive Him away. He is close to the brokenhearted, no matter their title or station.

## The Cost of Service

Jesus Himself suffered. He knows what it means to serve without recognition. He knew rejection. He knew exhaustion. He wept. Yet, He offers Himself not only as *Savior*—but as *Companion*.

Behind the badge, inside the uniform, beneath the collar or robe—are people fighting to hold their families together while holding the peace of the city or nation in one hand, and their personal trauma in the other. Behind the pulpit are leaders offering hope to others—while quietly starving for the very same hope themselves.

# The Cost of Service

## Chapter Four
### Invisible Wounds

> "The paradox of trauma is that it has both the power to destroy and the power to transform and resurrect."
>
> Peter A. Levine

You see no scars on our faces. There are no bandages, casts, or crutches in sight. Yet, many in the military, law enforcement,

**"Trauma does not always come with a headline."**

and ministry limp through life. These are the hidden wounds—wounds that do not bleed yet continue to ache. Wounds not stitched up in an emergency room, but etched deep into the soul. Trauma. Moral injury. The long-term psychological tolls—these are the untold costs of service. We wound deep and heal slow. Too often, we carry it all alone.

Trauma does not always come with a headline. It might be the explosion, the firefight, the active shooter call, or the church member who suddenly commits suicide. But it is also the sum of a thousand quieter moments, each one engraving its weight into the mind.

## The Cost of Service

For the soldier, trauma may take the shape of relentless images—friends lost in battle, decisions made under fire, and the fog of war that never clears. Combat may end, but for many veterans, the war rages on inside.

For the police officer, trauma is the slow erosion of peace—answering calls about car crashes and lifeless children, performing CPR that doesn't work, and being the first to witness humanity at its most broken. In this line of work, every radio call can be a life changer—or a life taker.

For the minister, trauma may not always stem from a single event, but it is no less real. It often comes from witnessing generational pain, chronic illness, miscarriages, abuse, suicide attempts, and deep spiritual desolation. Sometimes, the trauma is rooted in betrayal—whether through trusted leaders who fall from grace or a church that turns on its own ministry.

I remember a time when my choir director briefly stepped down, and I was asked to serve as the acting director. I was given control over the music department's budget, song

## The Cost of Service

selection, and scheduling. Although my predecessor was compensated, I received no pay, even while working a full-time job at the sheriff's office. During that season, a few choir members left because of my song choices, which leaned more toward a gospel flair. One member's husband even approached me and said I was wrong for selecting "those types" of songs for worship. "Those types" included songs by Kirk Franklin.

In that same period, I had to speak with a choir member about their conduct. I was then called into the pastor's office—this time joined by the music director I was filling in for. I was told that the role I had stepped into was never intended to include counseling or correcting choir members. In other words, I was allowed to oversee the budget, choose songs, and manage the rehearsal schedule—but not to address disruptive behavior. It was disheartening to realize I was trusted with the labor-intensive parts of the role, yet not considered qualified to handle its most vital responsibility: people.

After much prayer, I informed the director that I was

## The Cost of Service

respectfully stepping down from all leadership roles in the choir. However, I would remain a musician, as God had not released me from that part of my calling. The director asked, "What are we supposed to learn from this?" I replied honestly and respectfully, "I don't know." In that moment, it seemed my decision—made in prayer and peace—was being interpreted as a deliberate effort to teach the church a lesson. That was never my intention. I believe God gave me peace about stepping down so that I wouldn't walk away from the music ministry entirely. Truthfully, that's what I personally wanted to do—leave it all behind. But God, in His mercy, anchored me to what He had not yet released me from.

This was an individual hurt I experienced. It is not shared to provoke or promote discourse, but rather to offer a real-life example of the emotional toll certain situations can take when left unaddressed. Do not fall into this trap. John Bevere writes in his book *The Bait of Satan* that some believers are unable to function in their calling because of unresolved hurts and offenses (Bevere, 2014). I had experienced a hurt—but in order for healing to begin, I had to acknowledge it. A well-respected mentor of mine, Kim McDuffie, once said, "There are no returns on the things we carry for the rest of our lives."

Untreated trauma can cause the heart to grow either hardened or unglued. Some people shut down. Others live in a constant state of vigilance. Many simply learn to function while carrying it. Separate from trauma, but often interwoven with it, is moral injury.

Moral injury occurs when a person's core moral identity is violated—by their own actions, the actions of others, or commands they have given or received (King & Hawkins, 2023). King and Hawkins (2023) also state this injury can also stem from witnessing, failing to prevent, or being forced to participate in acts that transgress deeply held moral values. During war, moral injury may result from pulling the trigger, following an order, or simply surviving when others did not. The soldier returns home decorated—yet cannot look in the mirror

## The Cost of Service

without questioning their soul. In law enforcement, moral injury can surface after a necessary but soul-crushing use of force, or from the internal conflict of working within a justice system that often feels anything but just. It might come from arresting a mother in distress, engaging in a violent struggle, or witnessing corruption and feeling powerless to stop it.

In ministry, moral injury often arises from being part of systems that inflict more harm than healing. It can stem from covering up scandals, turning a blind eye to toxic leadership, or teaching doctrines that no longer ring true in the quiet honesty of one's heart. Then there are those who carry guilt for spiritual failings—marriages they could not save, prodigals they could not reach, prayers that went unanswered. These moments leave a bitter aftertaste, a lingering echo of failure, betrayal, or shame. When such wounds go unrecognized, they ferment in silence.

The consequence of untreated trauma and moral injury is usually a slow unraveling, mental, emotional and relational.

## The Cost of Service

Anxiety and hyper-awareness become normal. In areas thought to be safe, the mind is still on the hunt for danger.

> "The problem with wearing masks is that one day you will forget what you really look like."

Depression is sure to follow, particularly when it is compounded with isolation and shame. Drugs can sneak into the picture as a way to numb the emotional pain. Thoughts of killing oneself can intoxicate an unimaginable number.

As police officers, we are trained to run toward danger—but we are not trained to live with what we see. As Marines, they taught us how to fight, but no one taught us how to come back and reintegrate into society. When I returned from Desert Storm, there was no welcome plan, no transition—just a return to an unspectacular environment where alcohol became my support structure. I often asked myself why I was allowed to return when others didn't. It took twenty-three years before I finally understood what survivor's remorse was.

Some ministers preach hope every Sunday, yet they are internally strained and struggling to believe the very words they

## The Cost of Service

proclaim. This is especially true for worship leaders. I have stood before my congregation, leading people into the presence of God, while privately wrestling with my own beliefs. I didn't even realize the toll I was carrying—as a veteran, a police officer, and a worship leader.

Mental health care still carries stigma in many corners of service. As the need for support becomes more and more visible, calling it in is often still viewed as a sign of weakness. In the worlds of the military, law enforcement, and ministry, weakness, frailty, and vulnerability are often downplayed—or worse, quietly punished. I refused to acknowledge my own struggles because I didn't want to appear "broken."

These are worthy virtues, but weaponized, they are prisons. I had no idea I was being held captive by my trauma. I only knew real men never quit or show weakness. This thought was the biggest lie I would ever believe. True strength allows for the testament of weakness and perseverance while overcoming.

# The Cost of Service

No one ever wants to own up to the fact that they are unraveling on the inside. We are afraid to be judged, to be rejected, or be sent away. As a result, we put on the mask. The problem with wearing masks is that one day you will forget what you really look like.

The officer is polished, always smiling, but dreads every call. The soldier posts a flag on social media but hasn't slept through the night in years. The preacher proclaims faith on Sunday, while secretly plotting their escape on Monday.

The good news is this: wounds—even the unseen ones—can heal. Healing requires intentionality. It requires sacred space. It begins with honesty. "I am not okay." These four words can pry open the door to healing. Whether whispered in a therapist's office, spoken to a trusted friend, or shouted in prayer—healing begins with acknowledgment.

Recovery flourishes in relationships, not in a vacuum of isolation. Key elements are peer support groups, faith-based retreats, trauma-informed chaplaincy programs, and mental health counselors who comprehend the culture of service can do wonders. Trauma and moral injury hurt not just the mind but also the soul. Spiritual recovery often involves learning to see God not simply as a taskmaster or judge, but also as a healer and companion.

Psalm 34:18 (KJV) reminds us, *"The Lord is nigh unto them that are of a broken heart; and saveth such as be of a contrite spirit."* That promise holds true for soldiers, police officers, and ministers alike. Healing is not instantaneous. It is a journey. Sometimes it's messy. Often it looks like two steps forward and one step back. Still, healing is possible—with time, tools, and grace.

Henri Nouwen once wrote about the idea of the "wounded healer." This concept is based on the belief that those who help others through pain need not be completely whole or strong themselves and that their own wounds can become sacred tools of healing (Marchinkowski, 2023). Many who have fought and suffered are not broken because they were weak, but

# The Cost of Service

because they were strong—stronger than most will ever understand. Those who finally heal often become the fiercest healers of all.

## Chapter Five
### Faith under Fire

> "Tolerance implies no lack of commitment to one's own beliefs. Rather it condemns the oppression or persecution of others."
>
> John F. Kennedy

Faith is easy when the sky is clear, prayers are answered, and everything feels smooth. But what happens when faith turns to murder? When does hope collide with horror? What do you do when the God you've trusted in seems unresponsive in the face of evil?

For soldiers, police, and clergy, faith is not just a personal belief—it is a battlefield. It is contested not in seminaries and sanctuaries, but in sandstorms and sirens, in morgues and in sanctuaries that are no longer sanctuaries. The crucible of crisis either deepens faith or pushes it to the brink.

This chapter explores how faith is tested—how it bends, breaks, and grows when pushed to its limits. Soldiers at war

## The Cost of Service

confront the extremes of human experience. We saw the best of humanity and the worst—often in the same day. We watched comrades die, civilians suffer, and peace promises go unmet. In such circumstances, belief is both a sanctuary and a puzzle. I have seen service members discover God in the trenches.

> **"Faced with death and injustice, faith is a decision, an act of the will to resist every form of despair."**

I have heard it said many times before: *"There are no atheists in foxholes."* In the horror of combat, quite a few men cry out to God. Prayer becomes instinctive, not customary. In such moments, survival can feel like a kind of miracle. Yet others lose faith in the smoke.

How can a good God allow the bodies of children to be strewn across a bombed village—left for the buzzards to feed upon? Where was He when we had our greatest need? These are not abstract questions. They are the spiritual aftershocks of real-life horror.

# The Cost of Service

For many veterans, the psychological trauma outlasts our physical scars. We come home with a war not just behind us—but still raging within us. For police officers, the spiritual assault is less sudden, but no less devastating. Every shift is a journey into human depravity: abuse, murder, addiction, and suicide. We become so long exposed to misery that misery becomes habitual. We are trained to remain in control, yet we are not immune to spiritual decay.

Some lose faith slowly, in the drip of daily despair. Others compartmentalize it—locking belief into a box they rarely open. Some of us cling to faith *because* of our duty. The truth is: if we do not, we can very easily become the darkness we witness every day. For some officers, faith is the only thing keeping them afloat. Faced with death and injustice, faith becomes a decision—an act of will to resist every form of despair.

You might imagine that pastors, ministers, or worship leaders operate in a safer spiritual zone. Sanctuaries are not

## The Cost of Service

invulnerable to fire. For ministry leaders, it is a hidden battlefield. The collapse of church faith, the betrayal of a trusted elder, or the suicide of a congregant—these are the wounds no one else sees, because they happen behind stained glass.

Some ministers suffer spiritual burnout as human expectations and heaven's silence combine to collapse what was once a robust faith. Others wrestle with theological dissonance—torn between what they teach and the pain they witness in the lives of their people. Yet some emerge from these crises with a deeper, more grounded faith. Because in ministry, faith is not about having all the answers. It is about *endurance.*

One thing I overlooked with my trauma was the failure to communicate. This failure was one of the many reasons my first marriage failed. With my failure to communicate, it became much easier for my ex-wife to have the conversations she wanted with other men. While I was

## The Cost of Service

investigating drug law offenders, I was also detecting the full gravity of my ex-wife's infidelity.

I identified at least eleven men with whom she was having sexually explicit conversations—and one I knew she was physically involved with. That man was someone I had welcomed into my home. I thought of him as a little brother. I was even his mentor in the National Guard Youth Challenge Program.

Betrayal is only betrayal when those you care for are the transgressors. There was even one instance when one of the guys called the house phone and my ex answered the phone and went locked up in the rear bedroom. We were supposed to be leaving for church. She stayed home on the phone and I went to church as a "good, faithful" worship leader. After reading this. I know many have placed themselves and asserted what you would have done or maybe even developed an opinion of my actions or lack thereof.

If I were the rage-riddled Marine returning from service,

## The Cost of Service

I may have responded differently. It would have been easy for me to be like my father and break up some furniture but at what cost. A domestic altercation ends my law enforcement career and removes me as a worship minister. The very positions of service I felt called to.

With all these discoveries, the question naturally follows: *"Why did you stay so long?"* The answer is simple. I wanted to do what I believed was spiritually correct. I didn't want to end up like my parents—divorced. The breaking point came when I discovered new contact with yet another man. When I asked about the communication, her response was, *"What evidence do you have that I've done anything?"*

As a police officer, I'd heard that question countless times—from suspects I eventually arrested. I was not about to tolerate that kind of deflection in my own home. After eighteen years, I filed for divorce. That night, I slept at my narcotics office—unbeknownst to anyone. You see, even while my personal life was unraveling, I still had to maintain the

## The Cost of Service

appearance of strength—not just as an officer, but as a worship minister. I still had to investigate and close cases. I still had to lead a congregation in worship.

The one thing that is obvious from all three callings: military, law enforcement, and ministry, is that faith is built, not assumed. It has to be able to tolerate a contradiction: a God of peace in the time of war, a God of justice in an unjust system, or a loving God in a sanctuary where leaders fall. When belief crashes against suffering, black-and-white theology falls apart. The regular answers do not hold. Bible verses stamped on coffee mugs sound empty. Here is where faith is lost or polished. The Book of Job turns into a mirror as does Gethsemane, where even Christ himself cried out: "My God, My God, why have You forsaken Me?" (Mark 15:34, King James Version).

This faith under fire is not mere belief but is converted into defiant trust, and occasionally trembling trust, for it is no easy thing. Scripture does not promise that faith will protect us from suffering. It does hold out that suffering can purify faith.

# The Cost of Service

Romans 5:3-4, paraphrased, claims, "Suffering produces perseverance; perseverance, character; and character, hope."

This hope is not always easy to find. Sometimes, it takes years. Sometimes, it comes through silence, through weeping, through therapy and priestly prayers I cannot feel—let alone comprehend—because it feels like shouting into the cosmos, into a void. When hope does arrive, it lands with weight. It is not built on feelings—but on *faithfulness*. It does not rest in results—but in *presence*. It is not a comfort-born dream—it is a *conviction*.

Sometimes, faith under fire isn't about certainty. It is a decision to *hold on* when everything in you wants to *let go*. Sometimes, holding on means loosening your grip—loosening your grip on who you thought God was in order to embrace who He truly is.

A soldier may move from believing God should fix everything to realizing God walks with them through everything. An officer may stop asking, *why* or *where is God in this?* and begin to see God in the mercies— in small victories,

## The Cost of Service

in the partner who had their back, in the breath they still have. A minister may still carry questions— but no longer run from them. They bring them to prayer. They wrestle like Jacob— and though they may a limp away, they limp away *blessed*. Faith under fire is not weak. It is not blind. It is not naïve.

Faith knows the heat of suffering and refuses to be consumed. To the soldier weary of battle, officer tired of death and injustice, and the preacher who cannot hear the voice of God, I want you to know: your faith will never go unnoticed.

God is not intimidated by your questions. Your anger does not offend Him. He is not far from your pain—He is in the fire with you. In that furnace, something *unbreakable* is forged.

# The Cost of Service

## Chapter Six
### The Weight of the Fallen

> "Grief is the price we pay for love."
>
> Queen Elizabeth II

After death, there comes a silence—greater than any explosion and deeper than any wound. It is the sound of *absence*—of voices now silenced, of footsteps no longer echoing through once-familiar corridors. For those who serve—whether in uniform, in the pulpit, or alongside others carrying the weight of community and country—this silence becomes a ghostly companion. It is a presence our nation often cannot name, and therefore, it haunts us.

> **"Grief is the inability the show love."**

It is the burden of the defeated. Each death leaves a gap behind. In military ranks, it is the bunk that does not get pulled down for laundering the sheets long after the others have been. In law enforcement, it is the chair in the briefing room that is ostentatiously left empty and the radio call that

## The Cost of Service

never comes. In ministry, it is that pew that stays empty and the voice that does not sing in anymore. These empties shout in their silence that we remember, even as we somehow manage to press on.

The sorrow we feel when we lose someone we trained with, worshiped with, or served beside is not some superficial sadness. It is layered—with guilt, anger, and disbelief. We replay our last conversation and retrace the *what-ifs*. We think: *We should have seen it coming. We should have done something differently. We should have interfered—somehow.* The mind circles back—again and again—trying to wrap itself around something that makes no sense at all.

In the military and in law enforcement, death is no stranger. It is a silent truth—an occupational hazard wrapped in dignity. When a comrade dies, especially in action, the sense of loss is magnified by the haunting reality: it could have been you. Survivor's guilt settles into the bones like lead.

Rituals act as anchors: the rifle and the boots, the folded

## The Cost of Service

flag, the bugle call that says all it needs to say. These traditions shape grief and offer structure to mourning. They do not erase the pain. They only sanctify it.

For those left behind—especially in leadership—there comes a second burden: the duty to steady the shaken, rally the brokenhearted, and model resilience, even when your own soul is frayed. In these moments, we learn that courage is not the absence of fear or pain, but the resolve to press on in spite of them.

For people in ministry, it is different in some ways—but no less poignant. Congregants become family. The elderly widow who never forgot to bring cookies to the potluck. The young man who wrestled with addiction and knelt at the altar each Sunday. The boy baptized less than a year ago.

Paul Barnes reflects the Schaeffer Institute's statistics indicating 70% of pastors fight depression, 71% of pastors are burned out, 80% believe ministry negatively affected their families, and 70% do not have a close friend (Barnes, 2019).

## The Cost of Service

Barnes (2019) also asserts approximately 80% of ministers will leave ministry five years after graduating Bible College or seminary. The statistics here may seem alarming to some but the reality is pastors are human and subject to real human issues.

The bond between shepherd and flock is sacred. When death breaks that circle, the pastor grieves not only for the one lost but also for those left behind. Grief, for pastors, is often a lonely road. Ministers are expected to be the comforter, the rock, and the holder of hope. Their sorrow is usually swallowed in silence.

The temptation to bypass grief, to push forward without tending to one's own wounds, is strong. Suppressed grief is agony. It seeps out in fatigue, burnout, and the quiet questions of a soul that begin to speak louder than many sermons ever have.

In every vocation of service, there are sacred places where the fallen are honored. Whether memorials, locker

## The Cost of Service

plaques, stained-glass windows, annual roll calls, or special services, these are not mere symbolic gestures. They are essential threads in the fabric of healing. To name them is to declare that their lives mattered. To gather in their memory is to insist that their sacrifice was not in vain. To share stories of their courage, compassion, and laughter is to keep their spirit alive.

Grief is not linear. There is no schedule, no checklist that marks the end of the process. The way forward includes recollection. Healing comes not by forgetting, but by honoring. The death of someone close can shake even the most faithful. The toughest cop, the most rugged Marine, or the most seasoned pastor may still ask: "Why him and not me?" or "Where was God in all of this?" I have asked those questions myself in grief.

These questions are not betrayals of faith—they are expressions of it. Doubt is not the opposite of faith; it is often the very container in which faith becomes real. True spiritual

## The Cost of Service

resilience is not found in refusing to see the pain, but in fighting to see through it. Coping with loss does not require us to silence our questions. It calls us to hold them in holy tension, trusting that even in our grief, God is near—in the embrace of a friend, in quiet moments of prayer, and in the legacy left behind by those we mourn.

No one gets through this alone. One of the great wisdoms of shared service—in a squad, a congregation, or a watch team—is that community becomes both shield and salve. When one falters, the others lift. When one falls apart, others carry the weight.

The casual heart-to-hearts, the shared meals, and the laughter through tears are lifelines. They remind us that even in death, we are not forsaken. The bond between service comrades does not break at the grave—it endures. It is in walking each other home—through funerals, anniversaries, and painful milestones—that we begin to snatch life back from death. Healing does not come by forgetting, but by journeying

## The Cost of Service

together.

I believe there is only one way to honor the fallen, and that is through the living. Because they perished—in war, in duty, or in calamity—their memory rises up like a debt we owe. How we live from this point forward becomes our witness to their memory. We carry their stories. We embody their courage. We finish what they started.

In doing so, we are able to transubstantiate grief into mission and pain into purpose. The badge on our chest, the stole around our neck, the title before our name—these are tangible reminders that we carry weight that is not only ours. We carry theirs too. Not in victimhood, but as a banner.

It is heavy to lose the ones we love and serve alongside. Yet there is a deeper, more difficult, but profound gift: loss reminds us of love. Grief is an echo in the heart, longing for connection. We mourn because we have loved deeply. One of my spiritual fathers, Bishop Ronnie Melancon, once told me, in one of my most trying seasons of life, "Grief is the inability to

## The Cost of Service

show love." I still hold that statement to be deeply true.

Yet, over time, as the tears happen less often, and the memories begin to hurt less, we are left changed by the people we lost. They are our leaders and we look to them. Their courage, our standard and their service, our inspiration.

We will lose people in this life. Some will be gone in an instant; others, after long and painful struggles. Some losses we will anticipate. Others will take us by surprise. In every loss, there is also a calling—a summons not only to grieve but to live more deeply. To live more deeply is to love more fiercely, to serve more faithfully, and to remember more fully. For in the end, the burden of the fallen is not one to be cast aside lightly. It is a weight to be carried—solemnly, purposefully, and with light.

# The Cost of Service

## Chapter Seven

### Families on the Front Line

> "Families are the compass that guide us. They are the inspiration to reach great heights, and our comfort when we occasionally falter."
>
> Brad Henry

For many, the calling to be a peace officer, service member, or minister is a badge of honor and deep dedication. Behind every badge, uniform, and pulpit are families who quietly bear the emotional and psychological weight of that call.

**"The risk is inherent in these types of occupations."**

Spouses, children, and loved ones stand on the front lines of concern, sacrifice, and emotional endurance.

This chapter explores the often-unspoken cost of service on these families—and the extraordinary strength required to live in the shadow of duty.

Bowles et al. (2015) describe families as a source of support critical to the foundation of total family fitness. Families of police officers, ministers, and military members

## The Cost of Service

often live in a dual reality. Spouses of those in these professions find themselves living in the shadow of individuals the world hails as heroes. While their partners are celebrated, they are often left grappling with absence, strain, and the daily uncertainty that comes with the job. They are the unheralded partners in a mission that stretches far beyond duty hours, infiltrating countless corners of domestic life. Their sacrifices are ongoing—and mostly unseen.

These high-pressure professions are often sustained on the home front by spouses who carry the emotional and logistical weight of life while their loved ones serve others. Law enforcement spouses manage the anxiety of night shifts; military spouses endure long deployments; ministers' spouses navigate the unpredictable, around-the-clock demands of caring for a congregation. They must remain emotionally present for their partners while quietly wrestling with their own loneliness, anxiety, and exhaustion. These roles require

## The Cost of Service

profound emotional agility and a deep reservoir of inner strength.

When duty pulls one partner away, the other is often left to step into both roles: nurturer and wage-earner. This dual responsibility can create imbalance, provoke resentment, and slowly deplete emotional reserves. Re-entry—after deployments or prolonged, high-stress seasons of ministry or patrol—is rarely smooth. Roles must be redefined, expectations renegotiated, and connection reestablished. The struggle to reattach after long periods of emotional or physical absence is an ongoing and familiar battle in these families.

Children growing up in such environments often develop heightened sensitivity to danger, a deep sense of responsibility, and a need to navigate unpredictability. A police officer's child may flinch at the sound of a siren. A military child might struggle with constant moves and missed birthdays. A minister's child may feel the pressure of living under the congregation's watchful eye. These children often grow up fast—

## The Cost of Service

but beneath the surface, many carry the quiet emotional weight of their parents' call to serve.

Risk is inherent in these types of occupations. Police officers face the threat of violence with every shift. Troops may be deployed into hostile territory at a moment's notice. When my unit was deployed for Operation Desert Shield/Desert Storm, my Gunnery Sergeant shouted, "Garner, you've got 10 minutes to pack your trash." With that, I grabbed my sea bag with basic essentials. Everything else in my room was packed and stored by others.

Ministers, too, live in constant proximity to grief, tragedy, and crisis—each one quietly draining emotional availability at home. For families, the fear of a knock on the door or a late-night phone call hangs like a storm cloud—binding them to their homes and keeping children indoors. This state of constant readiness wears on the mental health of both the professionals and their families.

Routine is a luxury for many of these households.

# The Cost of Service

Sudden schedule changes, emergency calls, and deployments make planning feel fragile, if not futile. Families learn to be flexible—but that flexibility comes at a price. The absence of consistent routine makes it difficult to build traditions or maintain a sense of normalcy, especially for children who crave structure and predictability.

Support networks—whether extended family, faith communities, or peer groups—are vital. Yet many families still feel isolated by the specific challenges they face. Law enforcement families may be met with suspicion or distrust from their communities. Military families are often physically distanced from extended support systems. Ministry families can struggle with confidentiality, blurred boundaries, and the unique pressures of spiritual leadership. Even when support is available, pride, privacy concerns, or a lack of understanding may prevent families from reaching for it.

Faith can be both a refuge and a resource. For many families, prayer, worship, and Scripture provide grounding in

## The Cost of Service

the midst of chaos. Faith gives purpose to sacrifice and frames hardship as part of a higher calling. This is especially true for the families of ministers, who often rely on their spiritual foundation to navigate the stresses of public life and the weight of spiritual responsibility. Faith does not remove pain—it transforms it.

Consistent, open communication within families is essential. It can be difficult—especially for men in law enforcement or the military—to talk about the experiences they carry. For ministers, the challenge can be even greater, as their struggles are often expected to remain hidden. When I returned from the Middle East, I hardly spoke at all. I did not share what I had seen, what I felt, or what I feared. I believed that vulnerability was weakness. But through both group and individual counseling, I came to understand that vulnerability is, in fact, the foundation of trust. Families who make space for emotional truthfulness—even in small doses—are better equipped to withstand the relationship strain that accompanies

# The Cost of Service

lives of service.

Tragedy sometimes strikes. A line-of-duty death, a deployment gone wrong, or burnout that leads to moral failure can devastate a family. Public scrutiny, ceremonial obligations, and community expectations only intensify the pain. Widows and orphans are left to gather the pieces of their shattered lives—grieving deeply while often lacking the support they desperately need. This season of loss demands a kind of strength no one ever anticipates having to summon.

It is crucial to acknowledge the sustaining role families play in service professions. We are, however, failing—deeply and repeatedly—to properly honor and support them. Mental health services, respite care, scholarships, and public recognition are not luxuries; they are necessities. These acts do more than show appreciation—they strengthen a family's connection to the larger mission of service.

Agencies, churches, and military commands must cultivate a culture that includes families. This means fostering

# The Cost of Service

transparency, offering family education, providing easy access to counseling, and modeling leadership that values balance and self-care. Institutions that invest in the well-being of families will nurture a stronger, more resilient staff. After all, the health of those who serve is inseparable from the stability of their home life.

Amid the despair—there are stories of redemption. Spouses who become community leaders. Children who grow into advocates. Families that transform tragedy into purpose. These stories remind us of the resilience that quietly flourishes in the shadows of service. They are a living testament to the enduring strength of love, faith, and family.

Families on the frontlines live with a particular combination of pride and pain. Their sacrifice is real, their fight is deep, and their strength is indomitable. So much is said on Memorial Day and Veterans Day about those who serve our greater communities, cities, congregations, and nation, and yet so much more goes unsaid, unobserved, unknown and

# The Cost of Service

uncelebrated about those who serve them. I, as a veteran, officer, and worship leader, did not truly understand the necessity of familial support until later in my journey. Real support for those who serve means showing the same concern for their homes, where the crucial struggle for stability and love is waged every day.

# Chapter Eight
## Crossroads of Justice and Grace

> "Forgive your enemies, but never forget their names."
>
> John F. Kennedy

> "Accountability for police officers should be an expectation, not an aberration."
>
> Alex Padilla

The path between justice and grace is not always well-marked—nor is it easily traversed. It is a line we walk in law enforcement, a path we preach in ministry, and a code we live by in the military. Beneath the layers of ethics, duty, and outcome lies an undercurrent of mercy. How do we—as reapers of discipline and keepers of souls—hold the tension between accountability and forgiveness?

That is the dilemma this chapter seeks to address: the profound conflict that emerges when justice comes face to face with grace—when the demand for fairness and accountability collides with the offer of forgiveness and

# The Cost of Service

restoration. In that collision, we glimpse the heart and soul of service professions—and the people who stand at their

**"Too frequently we give grace outward and save condemnation inward."** intersection. Accountability is the price of admission in these fields. Police officers take oaths to uphold the law. Ministers are called to uphold spiritual integrity. I served in the military, where justice, honor, discipline, and mission accomplishment are governed by strict codes. In each of these arenas, lowering the standard is not just risky—it can be tragic, even lethal.

In policing, the call for accountability most often arises in the aftermath of public controversy—when officers violate the law or use force unjustifiably. Internal affairs investigations, body cameras, and public oversight exist to ensure that those who wear the badge do not dishonor its meaning. Yet, even among the best of us, there remains a lingering fear of failure—a heavy, uncomfortable sense of responsibility, and the dark shadow of potential blame.

# The Cost of Service

In ministry, accountability transcends legal boundaries and enters the spiritual realm—but it is no less serious. When a pastor abuses power, when a church leader falls, the damage is both deeply personal and widely felt. Congregations reel. Faith is shaken and ironically, grace becomes both the balm that heals and the standard that was violated.

In the military, the consequences of action—or inaction—are often measured in lives. Commanders must be held accountable for their decisions. Enlisted service members operate under the Uniform Code of Military Justice, where disobedience, refusal to follow lawful orders, or failure to act can result in court-martial or "office hours." The military is a deeply honorable institution, yet it remains constantly tested—in the crucible of conflict and by the fallibility of human beings.

Yet in all these professions, we find people striving for grace. Police chaplains pray with officers after a shooting. Commanders weep quietly at memorials for their fallen troops. Wayward souls seek forgiveness, aided by pastors who are themselves on a journey toward grace.

The summons to grace is not an invitation to sweep wrongdoing under the proverbial rug. It is a call to confront failure with honesty, to hold space for human frailty, and to remain open to redemption. Grace says, "I see what you did, and I still see you." This is not easy. In fact, it can feel like a miscarriage of justice. Victims cry out for vindication. The tension between justice and grace remains raw, complex, and deeply human.

Systems demand integrity. Public confidence relies on the belief that wrongdoing will be held accountable. In this instance, grace reminds us that we are more than our worst moments. It opens a door that quietly declares; you are not beyond saving.

Consider the law enforcement officer who shoots a suspect in the line of duty. It is a heavy burden—even when the action is justified. Typically, there is an administrative investigation, possibly a public protest or two, and always a

## The Cost of Service

psychological cost. The officer may experience two conflicting realities: the necessity of justifying their actions, and the quiet agony of having taken a life. I can tell you from experience: taking—or being responsible for—the loss of life extracts something from you. What it takes, you will never fully recover.

What does forgiveness in this context look like? It could be the community opting to view the officer as a human being, not just a cog in the machine. It could be the officer forgiving themselves, not as a delusional way of abdicating responsibility, but as the first step in the healing process.

Think of the military commander who orders men into a fatal ambush. It is possible there were intelligence failures. Perhaps the threat was ultimately underestimated. The sorrow that follows is incalculable. The responsibility can take the form of debriefs, reprimands, or even transfer. On the inside, that leader continues to grapple with ghosts. Here, grace can resemble the parents of the troops saying, "We do not blame you," or a minister responding, "God's mercy covers even this."

## The Cost of Service

In ministry, the dynamic is often reversed. Even though a minister has to continue holding people accountable, they are also the ones that must be willing to extend forgiveness to the addict, adulterer, or abuser. How do you tell someone they are both welcome in church, but they would never be able to serve in leadership because of their actions? How do you teach mercy without making excuses for harm? The answer is in courageous clarity; naming the wrong, and extending the hand of grace.

Restorative—not retributive—justice is the just punishment. Its aim is to make things right, not simply to inflict pain. This is where grace enters the picture. Grace does not eliminate the need for consequences; it redeems them. It allows justice to do its job without erasing the humanity of the one who has gone astray.

In law enforcement, this may look like a balance of discipline and counseling. In the military, it might involve both punishment and support from the community. In ministry, the process of discipline and restoration—often referred to as church

## The Cost of Service

discipline—is followed by the painstaking and redemptive work of rebuilding trust and integrity.

The sad truth is that not everyone wants grace. Some prefer vengeance over redemption. Some wrongdoers reject grace even when it is extended. For those who receive it, grace becomes a lifeline. It does not overwrite the past—it gives the past meaning.

Then there is the final, often overlooked challenge: How do those in these professions find grace for themselves? The police officer who lies awake, haunted. The minister struggling with their own faith. The soldier who cannot forget the face of a child in a war zone. These are not betrayals of duty—they are expressions of humanity.

Too often, we extend grace outward while reserving condemnation for ourselves. Ministers burn out quietly. Officers drink alone. Soldiers isolate. If grace is to mean anything, it must begin with recognizing that those who protect and serve, who preach and lead, who fight and follow—are not

# The Cost of Service

machines. They are human beings, just as in need of forgiveness as those they so often offer it to.

To live at the intersection of justice and grace is not to resolve the tension—it is to dwell faithfully within it. It is to say, "You were wrong," and also, "You are loved." It is knowing when to declare, "This behavior must be corrected," and when to affirm, "This soul must be restored."

It means staring into the eyes of broken systems without becoming broken ourselves. It is holding the line and holding the hand. It is being strong enough to discipline, and gentle enough to forgive. In a world that often demands we choose either justice or grace, our vocation calls us to something deeper—and more sacred. We must carry both.

Justice and grace are sacred space at which we stand at the crossroads. It is where we kneel to reflect, where we gently lay down our ego and then pick up compassion, where we speak the truth without flinching, but also without wielding it like a weapon. In our trades and in our different professions we

# The Cost of Service

must elect not only who we are every day, but who we are to become. It is not an easy road. It is a righteous one.

# The Cost of Service

## Chapter Nine
### When the Mission Ends

> "No one can live without relationship. You may withdraw into the mountains, become a monk, a sannyasi, wander off into the desert by yourself, but you are related. You cannot escape from that absolute fact. You cannot exist in isolation."
>
> Jiddu Krishnamurti

One day, the mission ends—whether planned or abrupt.

The last patrol. The final deployment. The closing sermon. The **"Where a service career ends, there is often a kind of grief without a ritual."** uniform, once worn with pride, is folded and tucked away on a shelf. The radio falls silent. The orders stop. The once-relentless phone calls fade into stillness. What comes next is not just retirement or resignation. It is a reckoning. A quiet, sometimes jarring confrontation with a version of yourself that no longer fits the world outside the setting where it was forged.

The end of service—for police officers, military members, and ministers—is one of the most disorienting chapters of life. These are not merely jobs; they are callings. They shape identity, establish routine, and forge deeply personal

## The Cost of Service

connections. Even in the best of circumstances, when the journey concludes, it often leaves behind little more than silence.

This chapter explores the psychological, emotional, and spiritual weight of leaving the service. It is about endings—but more importantly, it is about what comes after.

Service professions have a unique way of blurring the line between role and self. You do not simply *do* police work—you *are* a cop. You are not just preaching the gospel—you *are* a pastor. You do not just fight for your country—you *are* a soldier. In my case, a Marine is always a Marine. Over time, that role-identity becomes a kind of armor—a protective layer that shields against both external pressure and internal vulnerability. But what happens when that armor is no longer needed?

For many officers, retirement is not a relief—it is an unraveling. The badge was not just a symbol of authority; it was a mirror reflecting the person they believed themselves to be. Without it, they struggle to see clearly who they are. The same

# The Cost of Service

is true for pastors stepping down from decades of pulpit ministry, or veterans returning home to a civilian world that no longer makes sense.

The earliest steps in transition often include denial or distraction. It is easier to stay busy, to bury emotion in activity, than to face the quiet question echoing in the soul: *Who am I now?* We often justify this by telling ourselves we have earned a break or will enjoy the silence. Beneath that language there is often the deeper truth that some do not know who they are.

All these professions provide more than a paycheck; they provide a tribe. For those in law enforcement, that tribe is forged in squad cars and briefing rooms, bonded by shared danger and dark humor. For soldiers, it is the unit—men and women welded together by mission, deprivation, and mutual survival. For ministers, the tribe is made up of colleagues, staff, and the congregation that once waited for their words, leaned on their presence, and walked through life alongside them. Losing that tribe can feel devastating. It is not just the work that

## The Cost of Service

ends—it is the community that held you.

One officer once likened retirement to "suddenly being the only person in the world who speaks your language." As a Marine, I often feel there are only two kinds of people who truly understand what I have done: those still in uniform and those who were there with me. A pastor may know the feeling of no one calling anymore—of suddenly going from a spiritual father to a forgotten man in the blink of an eye.

The camaraderie, the shared lingo, the inside jokes, and the sense of mission—these are not easily replaced. When those things vanish, isolation sets in. For many who've spent years in the thick of it—pursuing suspects, preaching sermons, or commanding troops—the silence of life after service can feel unnatural, even unbearable. The quiet becomes intrusive.

The adrenaline is gone. The urgency is gone. What remains is often a haunting, existential loss of purpose. The days stretch long. The nights feel longer and more restless.

Some drown themselves in alcohol. Others seek

## The Cost of Service

distractions to numb the void. Still others sink into depression—not because of what they saw during service, but because of what followed: the silence, the emptiness, the absence of meaning. The logistical shift becomes an emotional and spiritual one, too. I have been there. I have felt the depression. I have tried to drown the noise with alcohol—and failed. The emptiness could never be filled.

Where a service career ends, there is often a kind of grief without a ritual. There is no funeral for your badge, no eulogy for your call sign, and no wake for last Sunday at the pulpit. The mourning is there but it is unheeded. For some, it is nostalgia, or missing the job. For others, it can be resentment feeling coworkers forgot about you the day that you walked out.

Some are left to question why they feel so adrift. This unrecognized grief makes healing more difficult. With no defined point to grieve the conclusion of the mission, the loss can become toxic. The identity crisis deepens, and many say they are starting to wonder whether their years of service meant

# The Cost of Service

anything at all.

If identity was once rooted in service, then the post-service journey becomes one of reconstruction—not reinvention, but reclamation. It means asking hard questions: Who am I without the uniform? What do I still believe in? What parts of me were never tied to the role?

This process is slow and must be done with intention. Some find renewal in mentoring the next generation—as teachers, counselors, or chaplains. Others pour that energy into their families, into community volunteer work, writing, or education. For ministers, it might mean serving as lay leaders, counselors, or spiritual guides in quieter, less visible capacities. The same sort of thing happens over time: a new synthesis is born: not identity in regard to role, but in regard to essence. Instead of thinking of yourself as a cop, have the thought that you protected people, and that you still believe in justice. Instead of minister, the notion is that you were called to love and lead people, just in different ways.

## The Cost of Service

The enemy of transition is isolation. That is why support groups are vital. Veterans' groups, retired law enforcement associations, and ministerial fellowships all have an important place in this journey. For those in transition, these spaces serve as a lifeline—a reminder that they are not alone, not forgotten, and not without worth.

These groups also offer room for meaningful reflection. They provide a place to talk about things that civilians may never fully understand. More importantly, they create a mirror for shared experience—a space where suffering can be acknowledged and where purpose can be reignited.

One such experience for me was becoming involved in the Vietnam Veterans Group at the VA. Although I had my own social worker, I was not truly able to unburden myself until I sat among others who had lived through experiences like mine. This is not a criticism of the social worker—the group setting simply gave me a sense of comfort and a freedom from judgment that I had not felt before.

## The Cost of Service

For ministers, the challenge of transition may be especially complex—not only an existential loss but also a spiritual one. Without a pulpit, some find it hard to pray. When no one is looking to them for answers, they may find themselves full of questions.

Police and military might also have to deal with guilt, regret, or disillusionment. They said they had seen the ugliest side of mankind. They have witnessed violence, corruption or betrayal. *Where was God in all of it, they might ask?*

We do not always experience spiritual renewal with ease. It needs room to grieve, a map from those who have gone before and frequently, a revisiting of the fundamentals: prayer, silence, honesty, and grace. Eventually, many come to see that their calling never truly ended—it simply took a different form.

The termination of service also impacts families. Wives who once held down the home while their husbands were deployed, on call, or leading a congregation may now feel the tension of a shifting dynamic. For children who had grown

## The Cost of Service

accustomed to a certain rhythm—or to a parent's absence—their unfamiliar presence can be difficult to adjust to. For some spouses, it feels like their loved one came home, but never truly returned.

Others feel as though they are now married to a ghost of the person they once knew. In these moments, communication, shared guidance, and a renewed sense of purpose become essential. It is not just the service member or minister who is transitioning—it is the entire family system.

The end of a career can feel like a death. At other times, it may feel like a birth. For many, what lies on the other side of service—though different—can be richer in ways they never anticipated. They begin to cherish time. They find joy in simplicity.

They rediscover their relationships, and parts of themselves long buried beneath the weight of duty. It takes time but redemption is possible. The mission does not end when the career does. Sometimes, the truest mission begins

# The Cost of Service

afterward—when the hard-won, costly wisdom becomes the lamp in your hand, guiding others who are just beginning their journey.

Life goes on beyond the badge, the uniform, and the pulpit. It might not be an easy transition. You could find yourself facing grief, disillusionment, or even loneliness. Yet, within that emptiness lies a chance for renewal, a journey back to yourself, a rekindling of faith, and a newfound sense of purpose. You start to realize that you were never just defined by your job; you are so much more. When the mission wraps up, that is when your personal journey truly begins.

# The Cost of Service

## Chapter Ten

### Redemption through the Call

"Wherever my story takes me, however dark and difficult the theme, there is always some hope and redemption, not because readers like happy endings, but because I am an optimist at heart. I know the sun will rise in the morning, that there is a light at the end of every tunnel."

Michael Morpurgo

How many officers are patrolling the streets while enduring a personal crisis? How many ministers are trying to steady the ship of the church while their own lives are falling apart? How many veterans are walking the streets, yet never truly made it home? I am each of these. But I am not alone.

**"Choosing to live in redemption is a daily commitment."**

This chapter is about what happens beyond the healed wounds. It is about how those who have given so much can begin to receive—peace, clarity, healing, and a renewed sense of purpose. Redemption is not just about fixing what is broken. It is about transforming it into something sacred. It is the conviction that even the darkest chapters of your life can be rewritten through the enduring strength of your calling.

# The Cost of Service

As a veteran, I was fortunate to have the Vietnam Veterans Group at the Veterans Administration (VA) as a safe space to open up. As a police officer, I have been both a proud volunteer and a grateful recipient of services from the Employee Assistance Program. And as a former worship minister, I have found support in church elders—but sometimes, it is necessary to speak with someone outside your congregation. I believe in the power of prayer. I also believe that God, in His wisdom, provides us with professionals—counselors, therapists, and support systems—to help us carry what we cannot bear alone.

Still, it is not always "socially acceptable" for those in service roles to admit to struggles—especially those that feel painfully human. There is a quiet pressure to appear strong, always in control. No one offers guidance on how ministers or officers should navigate these vulnerable places—until a crisis forces the issue. "Have faith in God" is often quoted, and it is true. But faith is not passive. Faith requires action.

It is no longer acceptable to wait for an answer God has

## The Cost of Service

already provided through His resources. Every act of service comes at a cost. Whether it is your time, your innocence, your relationships, or even your life—the weight of duty is never light. For police officers, ministers, and military personnel, those costs accumulate slowly, quietly, and often go unnoticed. Yet while the world may fixate on the price, that is where the story of redemption truly begins.

Before we can even think about redemption, we have to confront the aftermath. Consider the officer who has witnessed too many crime scenes, or the pastor who poured their heart into a congregation that ultimately turned against them. Let us not overlook the soldier who left a part of themselves in a combat zone. The end of a mission might bring a sense of relief, but is it true healing? True healing often takes a bit longer, if it happens at all.

The symptoms can differ widely. Some people carry the burden of survivor's guilt, while others wrestle with post-traumatic stress. Then there are those who live in a state of

## The Cost of Service

silent resignation where their inner worlds hardened under layers of emotional detachment. They go through life's motions, surviving, yet not really thriving. Redemption begins when mere survival is not enough anymore. It begins when you start to feel that there has to be something more to life.

The call that first draws someone into service never truly disappears. For a police officer, it is the drive to protect and bring order out of chaos. For a soldier, it is the bond of brotherhood and a willingness to sacrifice for something greater than self. For a minister, it is the unmistakable voice of God—urgent, compelling, and deeply real.

Even when twisted by trauma or buried beneath years of fatigue, that call can still be heard. It is softer now, weathered and wise, but still present. It no longer speaks the language of duty or urgency. It speaks the language of redemption. This renewed call is not about jumping back into the chaos. It is about embracing a deeper, more rooted purpose.

Redemption is not about wiping the slate clean. It is

## The Cost of Service

about remembering the right way. The scars of service—whether visible or hidden—can become wells of wisdom rather than sources of shame. When we take time to process our pain and name our traumas, they become woven into our stories.

Those stories have the power to heal—not just the one telling them, but everyone who hears them. During my time volunteering in Peer Support with the Louisiana State Police, I learned that I was not just offering others a safe space to share. By being transparent about my own struggles, I created a bond of kinship. In vulnerability, there was strength. In shared experience, there was healing.

Consider the retired police officer who mentors young recruits on the importance of ethical policing. Or the former soldier who helps fellow veterans transition into civilian life. Think of the former minister who comes alongside burned-out pastors, reminding them they are not alone. These are stories that have found redemption. The scars that once felt like barriers now serve as bridges—connecting hearts, building understanding, and restoring hope. In this way, the pain of service is not in vain. It becomes a sacred offering—a powerful reminder that life can flourish, even after loss.

For many, the idea of redemption carries a deeply spiritual significance. Faith becomes the lens through which we understand that brokenness is not the final chapter. It is part of the journey. Redemption is not simply about escaping our troubles—it is about undergoing real transformation.

In ministry, redemption may mean reconnecting with the quieter parts of your calling—the parts that are less about being in the spotlight and more about being present with others. It might involve stepping away from the pulpit and embracing a less visible, yet equally meaningful, role. Officers and soldiers often lean on faith to face feelings of guilt, to accept forgiveness, and to understand that they are loved—not for what they have done, but for who they are.

Prayer, confession, spiritual guidance, and scripture are more than sources of comfort. They are tools of identity

## The Cost of Service

restoration. They help us remember who we are, and more importantly, *whose* we are. Faith helps us realign with a deeper truth: You are not defined by your failures. You are not your pain. You are not your past.

The calling does not simply fade when you turn in your badge, complete your commission, or when the pulpit goes quiet. It evolves into something new. Some people discover renewed purpose in advocacy, using their voices to create change from the outside. Others return to school, write books, start nonprofits, or become counselors. And some quietly step into the roles of elders and mentors—the kind they once wished they had.

Finding a new purpose does not always mean making a big noise. Sometimes, it is about being there for family in ways that the job never allowed. It is about being available, not just on call, deployed, or completely drained. Redemption is not about getting back your status. It is about reclaiming those parts of your soul that were neglected or sacrificed along the way.

# The Cost of Service

The cost of service often lands hardest in our relationships. Marriages suffer under the weight of shift work, emotional distance, and the unspoken effects of secondary trauma. Children grow up confused, not fully understanding why their parents seemed so far away. Friendships fade—strained by relocations, moral injuries, or emotional collapse.

Redemption finds its way into these spaces. It begins with humility, with a heartfelt apology, and with simply being present. It is about the willingness to rebuild trust while reconnecting. Healing in relationships is rarely a straightforward journey. It is often filled with awkward moments, good intentions, and slow, steady progress. But this too is a vital part of the redemptive path.

The road to redemption is never meant to be walked alone. Pain often leads to isolation—and isolation can hinder healing. True redemption flourishes in the presence of others: those who have traveled similar roads, and those who are willing to walk beside us now.

# The Cost of Service

Support groups, peer counseling, veterans' ministries, post-retirement fellowships, and even online forums can all serve as lifelines. A thriving church community can also be a powerful place for reentry and restoration. Community reminds us: You are not alone. It confronts the lie that says, *you are too broken to be fixed.* It offers new ways to live, to love, and to lead.

To move forward, we must learn how to carry our past in a new way. Letting go does not mean forgetting. It means releasing the fantasy that everything could have turned out perfectly if only we had made different choices. It is about releasing the weight of guilt, shame, and regret—and choosing, instead, to walk in grace.

Many people carry the memories of lost friends, failed missions, or moral compromises like a heavy chain. Redemption tells us that we can still honor our past without being shackled by it. Rituals can be a great help: a memorial hike, a letter that never gets sent, a personal ceremony, or a vow to live differently. These practices create the space we need to

# The Cost of Service

let go, honor the memory, and move forward.

Choosing to live in redemption is a daily commitment. It can be achieved by letting go of bitterness, welcoming forgiveness, and nurturing hope. While it does not mean the pain simply goes away, it signifies that the pain no longer controls us.

A life touched by redemption can laugh again. It can find joy in quiet moments, create something new, and carry both happiness and sorrow without breaking. It becomes a living testimony to others: *you can survive this, too.* Redemption is not just a reward. It is a deep, quiet strength.

Redemption is not a return to the past; it is a journey toward what is still possible. The call that once inspired you to serve can now lead you to healing, mentoring, storytelling, reconciliation, faith, and peace. You are far from finished. The mission may have ended, but the calling is still very much alive. And in that calling, you will find redemption—molded by pain, cleansed by loss, and strengthened by love. There is

# The Cost of Service

purpose waiting for you. There is hope on the horizon.

# References

Ames, D., Erickson, Z., Geise, C., Tiwari, S., Sakhno, S., Sones, A. C., Tyrrell, C. G., Mackay, C. R. B., Steele, C. W., Van Hoof, T., Weinreich, H., & Koenig, H. G. (2021). Treatment of moral injury in U.S. veterans with PTSD using a structured chaplain intervention. Journal of Religion and Health, 60(5), 3052–3060. https://doi.org/10.1007/s10943-021-01312-8

Bevere, J. (2014). The Bait of Satan. Charisma House.

Bowles, S. V., Pollock, L. D., Moore, M., Wadsworth, S. M., Cato, C., Dekle, J. W., Meyer, S. W., Shriver, A., Mueller, B., Stephens, M., Seidler, D. A., Sheldon, J., Picano, J., Finch, W., Morales, R., Blochberger, S., Kleiman, M. E., Thompson, D., & Bates, M. J. (2015). Total force fitness: the military family fitness model. Military Medicine, 180(3), 246–258. https://doi.org/10.7205/MILMED-D-13-00416

King, E. L., & Hawkins, L. E. (2023). Identifying and mitigating moral injury risks in military behavioral health providers. Military Psychology, 35(2), 169–179. https://doi.org/10.1080/08995605.2022.2093599

King James Bible. (2017). King James Bible Online. https://www.kingjamesbibleonline.org/ (Original work published 1769).

Marchinkowski, G. W. (2023). To be wounded and yet

heal. How two wounded healers helped Henri Nouwen find solitude. Verbum et Ecclesia, 44(1), e1-e8. https://doi.org/10.4102/ve.v44i1.2839

Peterson, A., Chen, J., Bozzay, M., Bender, A., & Chu, C. (2024). Suicide risk profiles among service members and veterans exposed to suicide. Journal of Clinical Psychology, 80(1), 65-85. https://doi.org/10.1002/jclp.23592

Pollock, L. D., & Augusto, D. (2023). Protecting others, compassion, and sacrifice: The toll of disaster policing on law enforcement officers in the United States. Police Journal, 96(1), 83-102. https://doi.org/10.1177/0032258X211044708

Ritz, A., Schott, C., Nitzl, C., & Alfes, K. (2020). Public service motivation and prosocial motivation: two sides of the same coin? Public Management Review, 22(7), 974-998. https://doi.org/10.1080/14719037.2020.1740305

Violanti, J. M. (2022). Suicide clusters in law enforcement: a descriptive analysis. Policing: An International Journal, 45(5), 757-775. http://doi.org/10.1108/PIJPSM-01-2022-0006

# The Cost of Service

## The Final Call

You rose determined at morning light,
Laced your boots, adjusted tight
The badge you wore mirrored your vow,
To serve, protect and stand somehow.

Down peaceful bayous, hearing broken cries,
Patrolling beneath uncertain skies.
Each shift a prayer, each glance a scan,
A soul within the hardened man.

The call came in, a code, a name,
A moment sparked pursuit proclaimed.
No time to flinch, no fear to run,
Just duty burning, bright like the sun.

You held the line while angels wept,
With every oath you ever kept.
Your heartbeat echoed, slow and proud,
Until it faded in the crowd.

Now flags hang low, the sirens still,
Your badge draped soft upon the sill.
A mother weeps, a child won't sleep,
A silence deeper than the deep.

Yet in that silence lives your song,
Of choosing right, of fighting wrong.
Of being brave as others fled,
Of honor forged in blood he bled.

We'll speak your name in whispered tone,
A hero carved in steel and stone.
Yet more than that, you live in grace,
In every tear, in every face.

So, when the night grows cold and wide,
Remember you who did not hide.
You gave your all, your breath, your best
And now, at last, you're laid to rest.

You answered not this one last call,
But everyone, and gave your all.

© 2025 M. Anthony Garner

# The Cost of Service

## ACKNOWLEDGEMENTS

### Shawn Verrett Garner:

Sweet, I do not know where to begin. Thank you for allowing me to serve in the many community service organizations in which I do, and for always being a supporter of my educational and professional ambitions. You have been a rock throughout my mental health journey and a sounding board for all of my frustrations. I love you and appreciate you" does not seem to be enough for the appreciation I feel.

### Bertha P. Monic:

Mom you have and continue to be my litmus test for continuing to strive to be the best version of myself. Pursuing and receiving your graduate degree in your 70's is an example of your resilience for self-development. You are the example and embodiment of faith and perseverance that I live by today. The sacrifices you made in order to put your children in a position to succeed has never been taken for granted.

### Andrew Garner Jr.:

Dad there have been many things we had fundamental disagreements on yet in the end I realize I have learned a tremendous amount of work ethic and community interaction from you. Although you are no longer here, I will forever cherish my time with especially in the end and be thankful for life's most valuable lessons you imparted to me. Those who truly know me know, "I am my father's son." Rest easy Pop.

### Sis "Bea":

Sis "Bea" whom I will forever call "Ma," thank you for your wisdom, guidance and prayers along the way. You saw me at my best in ministry and my most broken times and consistently provided sound counsel. I am forever grateful and love you tons.

### Bishop Ronnie Melancon:

Bishop you have be a spiritual father to me in some of my darkest moments. You have watched my ministry evolve while

# The Cost of Service

continuing to encourage my personal spiritual growth. You have always provided wise counsel and your entire family have and continue to be my family. My spiritual path would not have evolved without you and I am thankful God placed you and many others from HOP in my life. Happy 50th Anniversary to you and Duchess and may God bless you with many more.

### Honorable Joseph L. Waitz:

Joe you allowed me to see the heart of community service through political office. You have continued to be one of my biggest cheerleaders throughout my career whether building schools in Uganda, writing books, producing music or conducting investigations. You have always been "you" in a unique manner and never changed your desire to help the public throughout your tenure. I am forever grateful to serve in your administration and more importantly call you friend.

### Honorable Juan W. Pickett:

Juan, you and your family, Bern, Jess, and Gia have been my family and I appreciate the advice, guidance, and endorsement for the greatest fraternity in the world (Kappa Alpha Psi). You have provided not only a good professional example but more importantly a great moral example. Your achievements are not just your victories but that of us who hold you dear. You embody ACHIEVEMENT and I am proud to call you big brother, familia, and friend.

### Jason Lyons:

Jason you have been one of the staunchest professionals I have worked with. You unknowingly continuously challenged me to become better at my craft. Your dedication to honoring the work that the men and women of law enforcement brought to the prosecution table always encouraged us that maybe we were doing some good. Your legal guidance has been one of the most critical elements in my career development. I am forever grateful to you and all your passionate work.

# The Cost of Service

### *K. McDuffie, C. McClellan, and D. Thompson:*

Kim, Chris, and Doug there is no way to separate you three. Each of you carried the torch for every agency employee and family member in need of assistance. Thank you for not only taking up the cause of mental health for our employees but also being influential in the development of the protected conversation law which will allow law enforcement to freely share trauma without fear of reprisal. Each of you are my hero and I hope one day to be an advocate as each of you are, to address the challenges faced by those who serve.

### *Sheriff Jerry Larpenter:*

Jerry from the moment you gave me an opportunity to serve on March 10, 1995, I have been humble and grateful. I have learned many lessons throughout your terms as Sheriff that will continue to be integrated in who I have become as a servant and a man. I still remember you coming to the old motor pool after I was only three days of field training. You ask if I knew the parish and before I could respond you told my lieutenant to cut me loose to handle complaints on my own. I was terrified but honored that you trusted me to handle the job. Thank you for the nudge which became the bedrock of a 30 year career. I will never forget you. Rest easy sir.

### *Sheriff L. Vernon Bourgeois:*

Sir, thanks for your support and for believing in my ability to do the job. You gave our team the freedom to explore new investigative efforts which allowed us to dismantle a large drug trafficking organization and show the true meaning of Cajun Justice. Saw what I did there? It was an honor to work under your leadership and I will forever treasure that time and your candor.

### *Sheriff Tim Soignet:*

Tim my brother it has been an honor to work with you in our years of training and now with you as Sheriff. We share a heritage of not only law enforcement but also we are Marines. Thank you for being genuine in all you do and trusting your people to do their jobs. You have a proven record of leadership in the Marine Corps, the Toys

# The Cost of Service

for TOTS program, and now as Sheriff. I appreciate all you do and thanks for believing in my message for training.

## Major Brian Charpentier:

Brian words cannot express the respect and admiration I have for you. June 6, 2025 was your retirement and the profession has lost a true warrior. Thank you for allowing me to teach in two regional academies you directed and believing in the subject matter. It has truly been a privilege to train young minds and prepare them for the challenges this profession presents. Also, thank you for never being politically correct. Your originality is what makes you the person of honor you truly are.

## Bill Sims:

Bill from the moment you defined NARC, you have been one of my most trusted teachers in "verbal judo." Thank you for the knowledge you have afforded me in learning our craft. You are the example of professionalism and leadership I have strived to emulate the past 25 years. Much love and respect big brother.

## Captain Derrick "Dawg" Collins:

"D" thanks for teaching me the tenacity it took to operate in our necessary but undesired craft. From the stories of the "Negative Infinity" to understanding the true aspects and utilization of following the money through forfeiture, you have been a most trusted teacher. Even when you did not receive what you should have received, you continued to be my sounding board and confidant. I will forever cherish our ops especially the "urban tomahawk" and tennis ball escapades. Forever your brother.

## Colonel Michael Solet:

Sir, from the moment I entered your unit, there are so many stories to tell. Whether it was you walking in on the team honing our skills in a game of Quake or you mistakenly trying to deposit my check, our journey has been storied. None more important as when I asked to go to a school to learn how to conduct financial investigations and you provided me with three (3) thick books of federal code and procedures. This was the single moment I knew

# The Cost of Service

dismantling organized criminal activity was my calling. It was this instance which ultimately led to the completion of a ten year case. Thanks, you for the challenge and push to look beyond myself. Also continued thanks for all you do for our lineage in the United Houma Nation. I will always remember the "do as I say, not as I do" conversation.

### Major Darryl Stewart:

Sir, I cannot begin to tell you how much respect and gratitude I have for what you have done not only in your career but as my commander. You had the foresight to press for the historic completion of a case I initiated and gave me every tool and constant encourage necessary for it to come to fruition. There is nothing that can or will every change my high regard for your abilities as a leader and one of the best interviewers I have ever seen. Thank you for your loyalty and leadership. I continue to model my actions after yours.

### B. Wes Hanlon:

Wes my brother, we are two that have taken roads less travelled and have been blessed to overcome. You continue to be an inspiration as you have risen above life's many challenges. From the moment I called and told you, you were selected to the unit to your later out of state years, you have continued to be a tenacious investigator that I have patterned my efforts after. We have made a lot of lemonade with the lemons life has given and I love you my brother. "Bravo Zulu" my brother.

### Martin Folse and HTV:

Martin, I want to take this opportunity to thank your and the team at HTV for your service to the Quad-Parish area and for your continued support. From airing my original musical composition as a theme song for your law enforcement-based show "The Beat" to allowing me to publicize each of my endeavors from music, writing, and community service, you have not wavered. Thanks for being our local media expert and for your dedicated service to the people of the bayou region of southern Louisiana.

# The Cost of Service

*To All Those Not Named:*

    To the countless others I have encountered along the way and those that work or have work for my current agency, the fact that you are not named is no slight. It is simply impossible to list the entirety of all those God has allowed to guide my career trajectory. I have been tremendously blessed to have many teachers, mentors, and colleagues. I have always tried to say "thank you" along the way and if I missed you, THANK YOU for investing in my life.

# The Cost of Service

## About The Author

M. Anthony Garner is an award-winning author and seasoned law enforcement professional, worship minister, and veteran whose life reflects over three decades of service across the military, police, and ministry. With more than 30 years in law enforcement and an equal tenure in worship ministry, Garner brings a unique and deeply personal perspective to the complex intersection of duty, trauma, faith, and healing.

Garner holds a Master's Degree in Criminal Justice, is a graduate of the FBI National Academy Association's Leadership Certification Course, and has served with distinction in roles that have placed him at the forefront of crisis and conflict, including combat military operations and officer-involved shootings. His firsthand experience with trauma, on the battlefield, in the line of duty, and within the sanctuary has shaped his understanding of sacrifice and resilience in ways few can articulate.

A certified crisis negotiator, Garner has spent years not only responding to high-stakes critical incidents but also supporting others through them. He actively volunteers with his agency's Employee Assistance Program (EAP), the Crisis Negotiation Team (CNT), and with LOSS- Loving Outreach to Survivors of Suicide-offering hope and presence to those enduring unimaginable grief. His compassion and dedication have helped fellow officers, veterans, ministers, and bereaved families navigate the aftermath of trauma and loss.

Through his writing, M. Anthony Garner explores the often unseen emotional and spiritual cost of service. His work sheds light on the burdens carried by those who serve and the families who stand beside them. Blending personal experience with professional insight, he seeks to foster empathy, healing, and understanding for those living in the shadows of sacrifice.

Whether behind the badge, the pulpit, or on the battlefield, Garner's life has been a testimony to endurance, faith, and the quiet strength required to carry the weight of others. His writing is both a tribute and a lifeline to those who have served, those who still do, and those trying to make peace with what service has taken.

www.ingramcontent.com/pod-product-compliance
Lightning Source LLC
Chambersburg PA
CBHW070521100426
42743CB00010B/1896